GODS OF INDIA

Shiva's Mystical Secret

SHUBHA VILAS

Lord Shiva's abode is the beautiful Mount Kailash in the Himalayas. His matted hair is shell-shaped. The ethereal crescent moon adorns his head. The waters of the soul-purifying Ganga flow down the locks of his hair. His one eye shines like the sun, while the other eye is as radiant as the moon. His third eye, between the eyebrows, is a blazing fire of wisdom.

Shiva's neck is blue because he had swallowed poison in his compassion to save mankind. Coiled around his neck is a divine snake. Shiva rides a bull and holds a trishul and damru in his hands. His awe-inspiring dance is called the 'Shiva Tandava'.

Shiva spent most of his time in meditation. His consort Parvati Devi had a lot to talk to him whenever he had free time. She would wait to get a chance to talk to him.

On one such occasion, she asked him a question that had been on her mind for a long time. Why was it that Shiva was eternal and she had to take repeated births to get married to him? She was Sati in her last birth and now she was Parvati.

When she put forth the question to Shiva, he answered her truthfully. He said, "I have gained the immortal status because I have heard the 'Amar Katha'. Whoever hears the Amar Katha becomes eternal." Parvati became very eager to hear the Katha. Shiva agreed to tell her.

The only hitch was that he needed an absolutely secret place so that no one could overhear him. After a whole lot of searching, Shiva decided that the Amarnath cave was the safest secret place for him to tell Parvati the amazing story.

The divine couple soon left for the Amarnath cave. To be doubly sure, on the way Shiva left behind his bull Nandi to keep guard and to allow no one to follow them. The place where Nandi kept a watch came to be known as Bail Gaon. Today, the place is called Pahalgam.

Shiva did not want to take any chances. After going a little further, he dropped his crescent moon and that place is known as Chandanwadi.

At Sheshanag he left his serpent Vasuki, and then Ganesha at Mahaguna Parvat.

In this way, Lord Shiva left behind his trusted aides so as to tell Parvati the secret of his eternal life. They finally reached the Amarnath cave where he further set fire around it to deter anyone from crossing over.

Once inside the cave, Shiva absorbed himself in meditation in lotus posture, sitting on a deer skin. At an auspicious time, he began telling Parvati his story of the secret behind eternal living.

But, despite all his precautions, there was still someone present in the cave. It was not a living being, but an egg sticking on to his deer skin, in which lay two baby pigeons. They overheard the entire narration. The fortunate pigeons became immortal.

Even today, the pair of pigeons can be sighted in the Amarnath cave where Lord Shiva manifests himself every year in the form of a lingam made of naturally occurring ice. Braving the rough weather and difficult terrain, devotees from all over gather here to worship the holy Shivalinga.

But what was the story he told to Parvati? Ahh…that's a secret we will never know because he did not let anyone else hear it.